C L A

MW01048459

The Conception of Winter

GOOSE LANE

Published by Goose Lane Editions with the assistance of the Canada Council, 1995. First published in 1989 by Williams-Wallace Publishers.

The author wishes to thank the Alberta Foundation for the Literary Arts for the grant which helped to make this book possible.

Some of these poems have appeared in: *Canadian Forum, Dragonfly* (USA), *Fireweed, Poetry Canada Review, Queen's Quarterly,* and *Tiger Lily;* and in the anthologies *Canadian Anthology of Haiku* (éditions asticou) and *Writing Right: New Poetry by Canadian Women* (Longspoon), and *Celebrating Women* (Fitzhenry & Whiteside).

Cover: *Naivete*, mixed media on paper, by P. Hurst.
Printed and bound in Canada by The Tribune Press.

10 9 8 7 6 5 4 3 2

Canadian Catalogue in Publication Data

Harris, Claire, 1937-
　　The conception of winter
　　Poems.
　　ISBN 0-86492-163-2

I. Title

PS8565.A64825C64 1995　　C811'.54　　C95-950168-1
PR9199.3.H37C64 1995

Goose Lane Editions
469 King Street
Fredericton, New Brunswick
CANADA　E3B 1E5

for

Conrad, Lennox, Joseph, Lindsay, Margaret

CONTENTS

TOWARDS THE COLOR OF SUMMER

that is the color of hunger
sliding off gull wings
hanging from nothing
before it slips
into ocean   drowns
in excess
the color of exploration
of search
sometimes frantic
sometimes lazy   drifting
dark
it hides behind faces
conceives
old age   winter
light
it surfaces in dreams
stranger stories
deep laughter
not the color of rivers
or stones   perhaps
the color of caves
or wombs
in deed   of future
immanent   blurred

*

Before a clear summer afternoon we wait
where tarmac wavers in unusual heat

through portholes   far off Calgary drifting
into sky   I close dark eyes against this plane

its subterranean rustle   the ebb and flow
of excitement   where atavistic fear pools

feathers and melting wax become sheared trees
the fateful earth leaping upwards   curious

I wait for the engines' sensual crescendo
for power to enter and lift   Far away

in my shuttered house everything dims
its breathing   books   ferns   drapes close

to their long communion   I go out as one
would who gathers in handfulls summer's early

peas intending to pore over them in a winter
kitchen   to remember then their first flush

and sweet green   Engines roar   surge   a minute
darkness   clouds   we watch the toy city slip away

＊

I become blue   meaning by this a measure
of release   what I imagine the soul feels

as it escapes drained bone   or pained
medieval angels suspect who long to escape

strictures   wooden wings/simple plane/gold leaf
into rosy form   and the fair   loose-draped airy

ease the renaissance frames   (those angels
whose skin would run blue-black   eyes slant

whose dusky pink soles would flash   and deep palms
lifting to sky draw the moon   are framed

in some distant future grace)   blue as in
the tail feathers of tropical birds I knew

as a child   or heart petals seen in tall shade trees
on long july roamings among the cocoa   bird/orchid

too far above ground for traps   in such blue
I float suspended   disguised in my favorite self

which blooms from my mouth   unexpectedly
in the narrow formal ease that is the people's airline

*

THIS IS A POST CARD
of three women
flying into summer

they sit side by side
yoked
to the fine delicate
balance of a friendship
they are disguised
as tourists

daughters   they
have shrugged off
the expectations
of others
which discarded   yet
cling to their feet

nearby an old woman
going home   a child
transparent
with excitement

but they go   three women
into the uncharted self   they go
looking out for each other
and following the blood
as one follows a river
through dangerous

territory
in darkness
camouflaged

*

A SMALL BOY   BLUE
seat-belt in hand
jiggles down the aisle

anticipation sparkling
in clouds of dark hair
in his eyes
he begins a hesitant
exploration

hedged on every side
nevertheless he steps
determined
in him tomorrow circles

a bright thread pounding
on doors

July 1, 1984

*

UNDER A RED BLANKET
twisted into a fetal
curl   engines
throbbing in my air
I dream   a raven

sliding down green sky
beak full of bright hair
where drops glisten

I am corded to a grey
street   looking up I
know   in a flash   something...
I begin to shrink

into a great noise
a cold sun   I shake
my teeth rattle   I wake
to a hand   a small boy's
gaze

July 1, 1984

*

EN ROUTE

An old woman   bleached
by nostalgia   bony
in long black silk
leans back in her seat
her hands newly manicured
trace in their thickness
the accepted gestures of a woman's life

her eyes closed   she
reels across her mind
home movies of her spanish youth

that have sustained her
through deep snowbound years
of separation   drought
a certain wild joy
and rebellion   even
death in clapboard towns
now alone and frail   wise

with a kind of success
fifty years on   still dreaming
she goes home   far away

from her children   their children
whose hunger for so much that is foreign
devours her
tongues knock against her sibilant silences

＊

Finally Gaudi's Barcelona   we slip from sky
like a hawk from blue circling   as if

the interval between arrival and descent
were unnecessary to find what we may be

in this strange growth under familiar skylines
bags tumble down carousels   grab at us

who are loath to leave the safe gleam   controlled
frenzy of airports   to become foreign   gibbering

tongues lap against us   we probe tired brains
for consonants   TAXI!   the driver's fat smile

the straggling city breaks   drags us into
sea-change   we nose into narrow lanes   tick

through a vague decrepit neon darkness   we swallow
this thick new element   we welcome the little death

*

RAIN WASHED MORNING
the whole city
sits
like an orange
waits
to be peeled

my teeth
my aching throat

July 2, 1984

*

ON THE ROOF GARDEN OPPOSITE
an old old man lifts himself
up   and trembling
pale sways with the wind

his hands gripping
the arms of his wheelchair
he stares down   and sways

as if in some high uneasy
place   he were testing
a bridge

July 4, 1984

＊

METAMORPHOSIS

Linked by delight we walk together
through Gaudi's strange gardens
brilliant mosaics   stairs   curved spaces
and light
already lit from within   we
become translucent

In these bright grave places
where everything is made by hands
where the palms are   merely
and lead to nothing   we make
simple   are girls again

On an avenue   columns going nowhere
in particular   we begin to web a forest
our bright dresses flutter
an old man comes to us   glittering
his hands held out like nets

Here where everything is strange   we
are transfigured   women of myth we fly
through darkness   balls   happy flame
We have no fear of our skins

*

GAUDI
having discovered
God's laughter
passionately
laughs with him

creates this worshipful
place   this cathedral
bright
with the petals of joy

and for his nerve
is punished
his great smile soars
unfinished

Barcelona   July 4, 1984

*

LAMENT

no one lives
in museums —
their ordinary lives
costumed
in living history —
anymore

July 8, 1984

*

JANE

cone in hand

on narrow cobblestones
in the old quarter
posing under a balcony
in full sail

those thrice endured youthful
paintings of Picasso growing
old in her)

is approached

the young guide
with the roguish smile   and
no sense of timing
gestures in flirtation

she joins the dance
with a certain energy
a skilled flamboyance

but her eyes are lamps
anyone can see her trim the wicks
rockbound   and lonely. . .

as if the world
as if all things rising
depend   on her

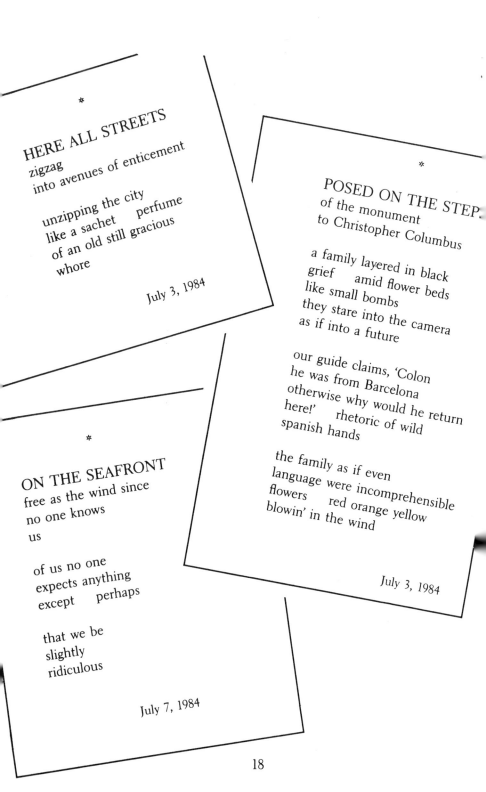

*

HERE ALL STREETS
zigzag
into avenues of enticement

unzipping the city
like a sachet   perfume
of an old still gracious
whore

July 3, 1984

*

POSED ON THE STEP.
of the monument
to Christopher Columbus

a family layered in black
grief   amid flower beds
like small bombs
they stare into the camera
as if into a future

our guide claims, 'Colon
he was from Barcelona
otherwise why would he return
here!'   rhetoric of wild
spanish hands

the family as if even
language were incomprehensible
flowers   red orange yellow
blowin' in the wind

July 3, 1984

*

ON THE SEAFRONT
free as the wind since
no one knows
us

of us no one
expects anything
except   perhaps

that we be
slightly
ridiculous

July 7, 1984

18

*

KAY

a cool spark to her waits
at the café table   surrounded
by that place
all its welter and weather
her bottle blonde hair   artfully
streaked with grey   curves a long
firm jaw   two young men lean
towards her   wrapped in such new
sophistication
even at this distance it squeaks

I sit at a café table   opposite
enjoying the game
I am remembering
the prim correct researcher reflected
in downtown Calgary   in angular glass
a woman of uncertain age carrying
a fashionable briefcase
with a long confident stride

cars hurl themselves at the lights
frustrated screech to a halt
safe under the trellis I sip something
long and coolly effervescent   rather
like Kay   I note how her past her future
its Eighth Avenue reality   here
in summer dream
is a dead thing lying on the ground

*

BEYOND THE CAFE DOORS
a mad boy
irrevocably   at home
in his depths

thin shirt
flapping
over long bare legs

his pure fingers
weave hard won tales
of love against
the raucous street

July 12, Barcelona

*

ON THE ROOF GARDEN
the old man shivers
in noonday sun

his fingers twitch
feebly at the blanket
stay to caress the wool

as if it were a dog
he calmed
or the past

July 15, 1984

*

JANE IN SUMMER

She sits on rocks above the bay   so still that were it not
    for the wind in her hair   or her blouse in its yellow
    silk blooming
She might be a figure carved from twisted pine   from
    summer   curve of her back and arm growing from the curve
    of land
At this distance Barcelona suits her   a certain grace
    black hair   pale forehead
Yet you would be better to think her a room rising
    out of ruins   a room put together stone by stone
Stones unfamiliar to each other yet holding together
    with delicacy   despite cracks and patches

A stranger passing by at dusk   looking up in softened light
    might catch a glimpse   shadowy elegances
From consonants of chandelier and red velvet chair might
    construct a language   a fable   might imagine skeins of wool
    tapestry
And a woman graceful in summer glow waiting behind leafed
    wrought iron bars
If drawn to rescue he knocked on the door it would open on
    a warm prairie room   fire burning low   prim French provincial
    suite   dried flowers near the hearth   a table laid for two
    the air expectant
But no woman there   nothing but an empty room listening
    for someone else to come along the path   someone known

Now each summer shaking off her year   its ruins   she comes
    to Spain   finds a new place to stitch and unstitch dreams
Summer after summer passes in an illusion of action   of vivid

21

life   rehearsing her stories   and winter
And always   like an after-image or a ghost the first Adam
    secret inviolate moment   the love around which her life
    still swirls
Imagine then the stranger hesitating on her threshold
    conscious in the stones indifference   retracing his steps
    down paths of rosemary
Should he pause he might hear clear and distant   the voice
    of that room piping as in a darkening wood

POSTCARDS

*

OUR OLD MAN SLEEPS
on the roof garden
his head back   his chest
if it rises   rises
too lightly to be seen
from here

above his head   two
yellow butterflies weave
an obscure pattern

were they dragonflies he
could read all his life
as one short summer's day

July 9, 1984

*

THROUGH AN ARCHWAY
glimpses of a crumbling
garden   a courtyard
and a young girl   black
braids falling over her face
her fingers mark
a forgotten history
while she stares
lips full parted
at the mystery/
at nothing
in particular

July 10, 1984

23

*

I seize this city as a woman seizes the man
she loves   wandering through it

searching out its secrets   pausing here
and there to seek reflections of myself

to break off bits   to take apart   to sink
my teeth into things as needs must

sometimes laughing at myself   my simple
curiosity   sometimes surreptitious   guilty

my bruised conscience so easily salved
by discovery   by surprise

there are times I sit   blind-staring
caught by the wonder   line/angle/color

here where an arch   a gesture can dissolve
to a door   to a dream   and let me through

and always   intent on the mystery   to draw
it out   to pry it open   as eaters of shelled

things present them to the air   then suck
them dry   to do this again and again and again

POSTCARDS

*

DRIVING DOWN
these quarried hills
from the heights
we come to ritzy
Barcelona
toasted roofs
high walls   pines
and jacaranda

'what would it cost
a house here?'

the driver'...
sacks full of money
cataracts
what am I saying
Niagara...'
his images tumble
over each other

from the back seat
giggling women
egg him on
to greater flights
the language
rolling off his
tongue
like a love song

July 4, 1984

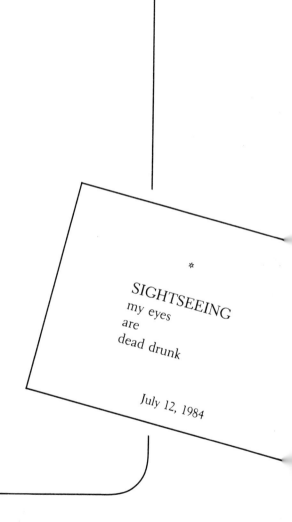

*

SIGHTSEEING
my eyes
are
dead drunk

July 12, 1984

*

Three bells calm the passing hour   a measured
clear-toned peace in Barcelona   I slip naked

from the narrow bed   slanted ceilings   I step
onto the night terrace   cool slate   stone pitted

rust red with the grit of ancient cities
to this landscape of roofs   dim wells   steep

slopes out-croppings chimneys   the weathered
expressions & dread hopes peeled to diseased heart

here and there shallow roof-rooms dim lit   wracked
stone heads square lives to cool realities

on this ruined dignity of terraces   of gargoyles
and grecian urns   I am stirred

would blend and flow with what is night
would become one with what moves in stone

all around like an exhalation the myriad ghostly
lives   ancient cities going down   then

rising again   generation after generation   ten
centuries jostle thinning air   convince

the future   what is human will rise again
and again   if only to sticks and stones

26

But this is not why we came here
three week exiles   we have chose to lose

our placc in the world   three women searching
a ledge for freedom   excitement   for self

(and I am here where the rivers   grief
and blood rose   think of it

where the lion's jaw crumbles   bearded by slime
its waters brackish   men with net and chain

and coffle may have drunk   kissed wives/babies
then slaved and died

their inheritors walk the streets   barefaced)
the night sky is assaulted by grids of antennae

west a crennellation of church towers   raised
above all a single red light   Four bells stir   fade

the silence is emphasized by caged birds   their sad
occasional night twittering   in the gorge below

a lone car splashes against shuttered doorways
a bundle stirs itself   goes back to stillness or sleep

*

A DREAM OF VALOR AND REBIRTH

My bed sways   swells to a moon
i wake wet from dull sheets
either this is dream   or the moon
counts out seconds
pushing them   reluctant   at me
its miser's nose snuffling over minutes
a myth wondering what more
can be risked from night's sack of hours
my life we're talking here
too scared to rise   i get up
immediately open and driven
now something formless   ancient
something urgent of blood calls me
to the streets of Barcelona
i cross against lonely lights at the Ramblas
stalls shuttered   cages open   trees
a blur deeper than night
the street nervous wavers   narrows
houses fluent rhythmical expand and pulse
breathless i am pushed and squeezed   thrust
towards the ocean   lights shimmer red/
green in rain streaked tarmac
overhead   moon glimmers white
before she settles in a nest of cloud
i follow a desolate nose through
dank courtyards   under occasional
arches dim sink holes of light
reveal aged eyes   savaged face
on a girl's still lissome body
before my eyes she bends into tender dark

shatters at my touch   fragments cling
here   where necessity hunts in pack
and each day   a tightrope walk over chasms
she has fashioned a parachute of lust
now her whisper expecting/suggesting disgust
crawls the air   a wind full
of salt sea   fish and oil   heavy with the wings
of gulls twitches in the trees
now i run driven
a cat between steep mossy walls
crouched in the darkest angle i wait
they rise: my mothers   clear pale
northern waters   my fathers   dark distant masked
forest fall   they rage in my veins
things rupture   bleed   separate
racked and purged
my tongue active in strange vowels

she steps out to gaze
sees slow swelling moon   tastes the flow
of blood and tides   knows centuries
knows nothing ever changes   in fact
there was never anything to change
in the end   rock and we turn through space to extinction
worms turn under the heart   and turn again
she sees me female reach for the hand
of god believing it must be there somewhere
in the curl of tongue or tide:
when i lay
when i lay me down
when i lay me down to sleep

and it is not

moon yawns a great raven   from its beak
a stream of heads gleam in street light
bounce silent on drowned pavement   flash
once   huge   before quivering to small grins
as at a joke too rich   too deep
for sharing   i move from them   pale
faces of whiskered albums   once
proudly displayed   i blunder
down the narrowing passage toward
something ancient
while brilliant flourescent dragonflies
swirl and cloud
the walls pulse   contract to a crevice
i think *not here*   *not ready*   stones keen
slapped into grey-green air and dawn
how strange it is   how silent
in the mirrored sheen of cars   i see
a woman   rain lashed braids cling
to the dark face   long blue robe clutched
like a shield   stubby plain toes   she sways
in a puddle on the boulevard as if it were
a convent hall   her wide mouth nibbles
the edges of this night
cars rush past to wild red-eyed quiet
the pale moon wavers
it is raining silence   umbrellas
mushroom under trees   walk through her
a group of girls run past   toss silent giggles
their clear plastic too small to shelter
them all brushes against her heart
their dripping clothes catch on her ribs
an old man shifts his pace   tramps
in his shrinking gait   beyond them all

a great line of palms   and flag ships
riding at anchor like a litany
there the Nina/Pinta/Santa Maria

the blue robe sways on this bridge
rough-hewn wood and darkness take
her in   rope grey   sodden coils
around her   the boat rocking
she rocks   planks groan
her stranded face opens on a ladder
leading below deck   waves slap against
this slave ship rising
she swallows the wail   stench
of men shackled spoon shaped
a miasma of fear steams from all
their orfices   yet their faces
black with refusal of such circumstance
nevertheless smouldering eyes welcome her
and their god gone astray in flesh
their god drumming in her bones
takes her by the throat
her cramped legs burn at the ankles
he gathers her   his mouth a wound
howling into hers

afterwards   a rage to survive life
choirs of sea birds   this god
fluttering in all my veins   fluent
on my tongue
from the ship's deck i see
the abandoned country   the moon
slides out of clouds into the ocean
slim   generous as a girl with time

*

LAZY GREY MORNING
cafe au lait
and fruit
on a rain darkened
balcony

the porter
braided and moustached
a fat grandee
raving discretely
against Madrid
extolling his brother
who went to America
when he was twelve
and is now rich
in New York

he serves *El Diario*
the mail   coffee
and   small gossip
which we drink
eagerly

his hand   cobra
quick
palms his tip
this small difficulty
surmounted
he bows himself out
while we watch
admiring   waylaid but
smiling

July 11, 1984

*

THE DOOR TO THE ROOF
garden   shuttered

July 17, 19

*

DEATH IN SUMMER

One known at home   our mail relays something of her
early summons   awash in the proverbial bed

its final currents strip her of luggage   she
nevertheless clings   I watch from this shore

four thousand miles away her desperate drowning motions
I try to decipher what works   what doesn't

how to save ourselves who no longer believe
in winged souls caged in flesh   nor yet

believe in shared rounds   in organic growth
and becoming   I shall drift through this city

alive to the possibility of this edge   if one
so vigorous. . . nothing   between me and the grave

I shall laugh   shall leave my stain here and there
dark energy of flawed creatures confused and clinging

to the bars   They say her face transparent under
the shock of black hair lifts with each morning's light

which she watches intently as if to be sure
she has seen

I know fading angels move through her as eagles
through the upper air

*

TO DISSIPATE GRIEF

we hustle in & out of shops
bustling to buy
everything
we say   'it
is cheaper here'
we point at things
weigh values
nudge each other
as goods are taken down
from shelves
or barstools
spread over counters
so we can finger them
dream their effect
tallying silently the cost
in dollars
we buy shoes & bags
belts   wallets   luggage
clothes with french seams
accents
dresses   shirts
suits   gowns
hotel rooms
a great shawl
we see our selves
transformed
strutting down closed
avenues   expensive
polished skins
on our arms
draped over shoulders

and this is what happens
when you die
first   you uncoil
the guts of pain
then you climb
where it leads
you gather yourself
pull yourself
out of nails
out of split ends
gather your self
into the mouth
a breath
that labours
a sigh that goes
on and on
because   this
is   it
your last taste
of earth
you want to remember it
suddenly   you are
and all out
to your amazement
intact
blue inside
outside   shimmering
made iridescent
by peace
even a species
of joy

we buy ropes
of pearls   stones
twisted modern chains
a watch   a pen
is cheaper here
saying it
we buy elegant meals
we argue for hours
over packaging
then buy gifts
prints   glass
friendships
bottles of volcanic
sand   cards
plays   figures
sculpted from
flesh
lava
dreams
we buy writing
paper by
picasso
records
T shirts   stamped
with the faces
of cities
and tangles
of shells worked
by primitive fingers
we use cards
tongues   whatever
coin is necessary
we keep lists

but eye hath not seen
nor ear heard
words lose their potency
and you begin to live
circling above
the final visibility
of your death
you remember
the cliches of a life
rendered remarkable
by dreams   by circumstance
and now   you
are free
of love   its tugs
its insensitivites
wild peculiar joy
of bodies
the landscapes
of childhood
slip from you
that clump of trees
that slight rise in the earth
those seas
that new land you chose
its particular weave
gone like mists
ghosts in this
brighter sun
this air
filled with being
you
now   one
with time

balancing bills
and friends
against ourselves
here where we
are free
and the dollar
strong
we luxuriate
buying everying
we choose
it is cheaper here

space
whatever there is
of law
settle in
and through you
no wonder
(we think everything
is cheaper here
all things
considered)
you know who you are

*

CONCEPTION OF WINTER

Sometimes in summer rain falls in great drops
heavy as loss   today
we see it black on ragged faces
on gypsy urchins crouched at the foot of columns
in this cafe   Not here spring's succulent promise
life like a peach
or even the thin stretched certitudes of winter
which we imagine as life   skin tight
drying on a frame nailed against a barn
in hot prairie summer
Only this rain stirring cliches   it dulls
the cold incurious eyes on bowed men sitting
under arches we have discovered
sailing behind the rundown facades
and unfashionable shops
searching a way east   it stains rusty mirrors
where our faces shift   and what is new and strange
quickens for a moment   We find a table settle parcels
guidebooks   order drinks   wait for the sun
But some gesture which haunts this place   something
in these women carrying trays of beer   and pregnant
with old age   reminds us of ourselves
We become sad   we walk apart in the wet aftergloom
of rain   know ourselves already seeded
And this is not the voluptuous sadness in great love
or even grief at our friend's dying
Just that here in this place   in our determined joy
we find ourselves fearing the birth of winter
We resolve to invent passion   imagine it as beyond
the circling of tongues   As the cold rage
which changes something

＊

KAY IN SUMMER

Someone   waiting in the lobby of a Hotel Imperial   amid
    the spaciousness   tourists   and peeling gold leaf
    might see it all as too hesitant for truth
Might think   for a moment   about the art in scattering
    too solidly carved tables   crowding too many dreams
    before dim victorian sofas
Might remember certain high-backed chairs   or a woman
    that could lend a touch of veracity to this place
From this   might wonder if truth is possible   if always
    and everywhere there is the notion   stage
    as true of a bed as of a lobby

Imagine now   Kay   as she steps through glass doors   and
    someone who glancing up   sees her suggest everything
    is possible   no   is probable in this place
Someone   who can tell from the easy music of her walk
    how decades and sophistication have slipped from her
    without a rustle
How she has stepped into these brighter softer eyes
    into this clear joyous laughter with out memory
Such a man now   iron-grey and ramrod   may welcome years
    hovering about her bare feet   scent of prairies
    songs of experience and struggle
May insist only on allegory: glitter and glass slippers
    smile on a killer toy

From the roof garden   opposite   our old old man ungentle
    in this summer night   gestures furiously   slashes
    at his wheelchair   a daughter burdened with wet sheets
    hurries to hang them
Then kneels before the old one to rub his hands between
    her own   until he smiles
I turn away from this   worrying its meaning   its small

38

beauties   tiny hungers and comforts   how like
an electric charge   the attentions of One

They step together into the leafy romantic air   and
    Las Ramblas   Kay   jaunty as hell   her summer affairs
    the sloe burning flame that makes autumn bearable
That perfumes her air as she moves towards the grave
    its slow   inexorable stages
Jane   flat in her deck chair   calls to me...She didn't
    come to Barcelona for love   love is hard   one wants
    something softer   only a little pain   a little grace
    and limited fallout...

On our last evening I search for the word that is resolution
    to her story   but she dances down stone streets
    shimmies in tavernas   spins in the dim light
    and that spurious lobby
Perhaps more allegory   perhaps someone watching closely
    will see her catch her lower lip between bruising teeth
    on the stroke of midnight
Now high above the city we stand on that terrace
    I am saying   Look   look where we are   the rotting stone
    the ragged haze from a thousand years of intention
    the avenue   those trees
Listen   she says   listen to bells carve the hours

*

ON THE BEACHES
such light   such pain
and   unabashed boun
of flesh

teased by this
We grow Picassoesque
angular   our faces
changeable

as masks

July 20, 1984

*

UNDER THE FEET OF HEROES
we three stand

you two in admiration
in white wonder

you talk   feats
of arms and passage

I see only the dead in black
mountains   hear only

the high pitched keen
of raped women   flaming

crosses   I stand under
the feet of murderers
of sodomites

July 16, 1984

*

I AM TOLD

the old weep easily   still
there must be another reason   beside
galloping age   why
as we walk together   this last day
full of summer light on water
I hear myself ask   what leaves certain women
thrashing   half a world from home   in the shallows
of a Spanish summer   with
out even the drunken grace
of sailors
you look at me startled   stopped dead
in the middle of Las Ramblas
to ask   are you crying
no   I say   looking up at you   no
something in my eye

beyond the school door
a butterfly free of bells
slides on wind

OF IRON, BARS AND CAGES

in	late summer evening softens angularities	*in*
half light	emphasises the roundness of women and hills	*the rented*
pliers	we four stare through drought dried grass	*room*
approach	to where below us the river deepens into black	*under*
the hair	above the brick-red massive rise of the	*half light*
the grey	General bears down on small dreams we swirl	*she*
hair	ice in our half finished drinks and sigh	*crazed*
the soft	women we sit as at the bottom of wells	*by the hours*
female hair	darkness and smooth sides crouched in cold	*of children*
that curls	we have only the strands of thin years	*trapped*
steel	to weave ladders strong enough to lift us to	*in the empty*
snaps	the round circles of sky yet like spiders	*pocket*
pliers	grown accustomed to dark we take a sensuous	*in charity*
tug	pleasure in the intricate manouevres of our	*drained*
naked	weaving we talk of strategies discuss	*of hope*
the mount	technique and image then note the passing	*calls out*
of her	glory of the year and steep ourselves in	*for an adult*
who asked	sadness what we would like is a rope	*body*
for a name	let down from the blue heavens from	*a male body*
who needed	that dark cloud shaped like a hand a sign	*any body*
only the name	on which we could climb could ride	*to ride her*
of a death	to an immense and furious life	*furious heart*

to every woman
                a season
and a pattern

OF SURVIVAL

                perhaps
what is important
                    is (to be
                        movement (in/ex
                            change
        •
so it was
from the beginning

            kicking against
and wombwall

                        at the last
before the plates shifted   and crust
opened my mother could not sleep she
walked   took to stroking her flutt-
er(r)ing belly   hummed soothe songs
took to gently smiling into air

                some thought her mad
                (
no good can come of it)

and never mattered what of me it was
that moved
                only that it did move
                            divesting

i   be

and all at once
              like hawk
motionless
silent eye
so i fell
so fall
        to this species of continuous
        birthing   always greedy at the dark
        breast
                                    (that first time   Great
Aunt Clem   her old alert night hands pause
to the father's gift of midnight cactus
its red moonlit flowering)

now i tear my caul with my teeth

dear john
so it is i sit on the couch
                        opposite
still in motion
this woman you tried to fill
with permanence   i remember hands
pressing my shoulders into stone
fingers   pitons   you climbed
in sunlight   your body
                        clinging for dear
                                    for life
your kiss   a precipice
you loved me   and also
as we love the small continuous things
the word *home* holds

you who chose to plant dreams

there were the mornings
groggy   sun pattern of summer poplar
your musk & familarity
what we love truly   the knowing
all of the other

there
      we think
              lies safety

on such
you based our everything
your dreams
              already in leaf
i couldn't breathe that thick
green air   i couldn't move
trunks so solid   roots
twisting through layers
deep feeding on the centuries
skeletal spoor of dreams
                        no
different

while you
flamed
in those branches
a burning bush

how could i not run
for us
flames have always been

without incense
our outraged brothers
burning
the fire next time
rubber necklaces
like spits
otherwise
hooded sheets
ropes
castration
and earlier still
fire in the brush
the net
the brand
and always hiding
hiding

still and all
your love   an impetus
or more accurately   a place
a station from   to leave
safely
so i did   and still
and all
i loved you

and
truly

thus
once again
            movement

that continuous in/ex
                    change
as in the beginning
i thrash
but now
            against the walls of winter
unable to sleep through the world
i walk   as my mother did
                        stoking the fluttering
                                    image
that we move through life like ghosts
intent on our own business   glimmering
in the aigrette of a total eclipse
feeling lost to us   and eating the earth
that we can pass bombs   like salt

consider this   and its casual revelation
a child   eight   suffers masked men
electric shock
her bound mother
screaming in concert
offers   any thing
            for such as these there are no mourning borders
who are merely our daily news   without prejudice
has winter settled about our hearts
who in default   no longer choose life
no longer choose   yet
                            from us
who are our own gods   prayers are not
                            enough
i have come to this
i would birth fires
see them as flowers bursting through snow

NO GOD WAITS ON INCENSE
for Rosemary

while babies bleed this is not the poem i wanted
it is the poem i could   though it is not that insistent
worm   it will not burrow through deaf ears
lay its eggs in your brain   yet it is all
for change
and it is not that beautiful weapon
it will not explode in the gut
despite your need   this poem is not that gift
it brings you nothing   you who insist on drinking
let your buckets into green and ruined wells   haul
in darkness   village women will lead you smiling
step back polite in the face of skulls
this poem will not catch you as you fall
not a net   no   it is nothing   this poem
not a key   not a charm   not chicken soup
and it is no use at all   at all
nothing at all
it won't beat a drum   it can't dance   it can't
even claim to be written in dust if this morning
the Bow sky-sheeted in light   the silver air is bright
with balloons   yet it talks from a dark bed
this poem   though no
woman can lie curled beneath its covers
can hide before boots
can hope to be taken for bundles of clothes   can hope
not to cry out when the knife probes
pray her blood not betray her   nor the tiny sigh
no   this poem   not even a place where anyone is safe
it can nothing   still nothing   still nothing at all
at all   in the night and disinterested air this poem
leaves no wound

                                    the moon thin

          a mere slice   diminishing
                             the valley
          the river also diminished
                   the trees   skeletal
                        a fine scattering
                        lights the hills
          this older moon   like
                        the woman
                             thinner
          held inside   herself
                   moving   surely
                        toward
          some final paring down
          the rest held in   shadow
                   still what is invisible
                        moves her
                        to that end
                        she must
          without embellishment
                   or fantasy

quiet village night
one lightbulb and fireflies
push against the dark

A GRAMMAR OF THE HEART

As earth lives the bodies of the dead[1]   she
lived language   at first she examined each word
skin peeled back   green flesh squeezed between
thumb and forefinger   till she tasted sentences
rolled them in her curious mouth   swirled them
around the sides and back of her tongue   waited
for the aftertaste   thin sound grew in her as
if she hummed   as if humming she sang

in here i
here i am in
herein i am in   and am
indifference
i differ in   here
am different her   and
in indifference am
within difference
am difference   no
defence   with
out herein
i am in

in this monotony   and as if she had absorbed
the word into her blood thus   it began to flower
in silence

---

[1]Luis Rosales "The Root", *Roots & Wings*, Hardie St. Martin, Harper & Row

Consider her   my mother   in her awful moment
my father's hand cupped in her brown one
his fingers blue at nails and tips
begun their slow fading
while she sits staring at that face
so suddenly frozen
into its final dignity
without a word she lays down
that hand   and as if she can
and slice through thick air to trap the core
of things   she closes his window
on the dense music of bees   of cicadas
of nameless life she draws his blinds
straightens his riotous blue brown sheets
pulls the heavy counterpane up   over his shoulders
then leaves him in half open contemplation
of what ever lay seized in his dark eyes
and shuts the door

How here to say the unsayable

when she was eight   death   wheeling over her
house   a great flight of corbeaux   of darkness
snatched sisters a brother   now deathbeds have
become her womb   from her first husband's at
twenty she birthed grief in black veils and in
honey   then her father died   she drew from the
hollow of that death the modern bread winner &
so fashionable   she laughed often   was young
her mother died   she shed the daughter   became
wife once more   and finally

If death knocked again she wouldn't answer

                              *

And yet believing in her own immortality

In something that is no more than nothing

Ravelling and ravelling her silences

Against death against offspring against
darkness with the soft crumpling of days
laying goodmornings and goodnights   one
on one on one   a haven   a fastness

Thus she turned away from us all
retired to her own womb   its slow
gestations
she lay curled
drank only when her body   newly parched   cried
out   and there
under the stigmata of her woman's life
she paced the deliberate   the walled moment
its love affair once tended as one
tends a garden...   naming
and with a certain ruthlessness
a certain awe...
now shattered   as by earthquake

For days she wandered among beaten
branches   among amputations and boulders
gouging herself among the thorns of hope
and strewn petals   till as if driven
from   or by a spade flaming into sword
she rose a stranger
the thing splintered in her mended
to a new shape
out of her clear eyes something   distant
surprised   looked on us

Now
through my writing window
the late summer sun flares
briefly
before his going down
                    (death   here   his wail still
somewhat in poor taste   a turning away
as from shabby defeat)   now
not silence   but the city's quiet
settles over the Bow

To sketch
one who discarded
words
with words
she was a woman
born in the dawn
her girlhood startled
by the first world war
she loved
she married
she buried
she loved again   married in rose lace and promise
then calm eye of the storm
she mothered
she cooked
she taught
she baked
she nursed
she danced and played and fussed over bruises
and laughed and prayed
and loved
and read
and baked   cared made wonderful punch
and yet
she was a woman who thought herself unwatched
her heart secret around the first grief   she
moved through her life as if she wasn't there

Through the plate glass windows
a lone plane floats soundlessly
Calgary's midnight wash of sky

no stars   never stars
a moon like a parenthesis

and still
i remember
how she filled the house with such quiet gaiety
gathering us all around her in the huge bed   in
the hot afternoons after the day's teaching   to
laugh at our stories
and yet
she wrapped herself around him   my father like
a second skin   and she fit   in the suppressed
laughter   in the chatter   those sudden teasing
silences from her room there was no space   for
any child
and yet
she was so gentle we rose each morning at five
to be almost alone with her   climbing the hill
to mass in the deep hibiscus dawn
and still   fired ebony at the core   or bronze
i remember rosary beads clicking like an abacus
in tapered fingers   and how cool she could be
how adamant in the face of certain griefs
and yet

She was a spell
a plot
i could not be like her
it was something
i could not learn   the way
i learnt
to make buljol
stuff cucumbers
match patterns
the way i learnt
a woman must have a profession
that way you aren't dependent on any man
and yet

now sometimes
i come upon her suddenly
and in shadow
now perhaps my grave's clarity
resolving itself
i understand
what passion forged the cool smile

Caught in the light of her infinite surprise   in
that silence growing longer than days   we panicked
doctors/nurses/sea air will do her good   forced
to Mayaro   she gestured away the days
our frantic whisperings
distanced even the clash of currents
at her ankles   we argued ways
means
how to live out a life refused
taking the matter from her gently
and as if it were ours
but she rocked the sandy verandahs
prepared bits of meals
as if these things mattered

and each day at high noon   she stood
in the spent sibilance of sea
at wind wave's edge   and day after day

I remembered my father   his sudden rising from
driftwood   a shout in trunks he strode into raw
sea without a word   steadily without distraction
until the waves break over his shoulders   he now
begins to swim further   and still further   into
brilliant sunstricken ocean beyond swell and far
breakers   his head a black dot dances where that
heavy pool of light becomes Atlantic   his head
grows smaller while our thin cries scratch   and
the gulls' cries strain above the waves
small crabs scuttle   flocks of chip-chip work in
aeons of sand   as if the world unspoken   were
still there

How she stands never takes her eyes from his head
the curve of his arm rising   never calling him
back   how he turns finally and many years later
how the world comes back   and he pounds towards
shore   and she   how before he can touch ground
turns away   as if the coconut palms thrashing
about her were the whips of scorpions

And wind   flares
from that ocean
strips from those palms
        from these river-green
poplars   the world's
wild   fiery
breath
now lean and dark   he
whistles
beneath my balcony

Where i have seen her   a wet snow falling
arms wrapped around her shoulders
rocking   as she may once have rocked away
noonday sun

And i have seen her make   from the space
between   a new world of snow
and difficult daughters

Once she said   a woman's choice limited
must be quick   and sure
her silences grew baroque

Still she wrote letters to the lawyers:
I decide not these children

in the windows
    dark waters of the Bow
drown a city

I phone my brother
the air
waves taut
with loss   he
says   she was so
gracious
did i ever tell you
he hesitates
suddenly gruff
are you writing this down

of course

In the end   twice married   rich
with experience of dark men
she turned to her third
seduction
death seeing himself invited
begins a slow flirtatious dance
and she with him
now like a young bride soft
with hope and mystery

And the present deserts her

as if the burden of grief had shunted her into past
tense she began to blur

i arched   found claws   spat at death   at fear

Eventually   cottonwoods stripped of their leaves
the Bow wearing thin frills of ice
she returned to that room
where everything was out of proportion

And there where even memory was too highly
polished   the curtains too heavy
she lay

And she was gone from us   slowly   so slowly   like
a sequence of gaunt ferryman   loved face growing
smaller and smaller   till only the hulk drifting
over the horizon   tip of a sail   For years

She wandered in a bright haunted wood   the dead
leaving victorian graves to call her name   small
sisters father husbands   she answered them   all
her voice   its words are a herd of douen clinging
to her skirts   their dead backward footprints

The adult gone from her in messy details   woman
poured out as water through a basket

She ceased to be the wall between me and the grave
yet   a cool gravity   an inquiring eyebrow

As transparent as an embryo

I would abort   but lack the courage of saline   or
solutions

And years

As if   or whether stabat mater were intrinsic   to
the mother

Dolorosa   and already infinite

Impossible to say her pain   or whether   for us
a wracking   a slow burning at the stake
i wanted her to answer   once

65

She lay   my mother   without speech
before a headboard too tall   too tightly
carved   my visits brought no softening
of that resistance   i joined you
i lay in silence   only your eyes moved
refusing recognition
and the shedding of your flesh was speech
when you had poured out all you could
i lay fat   unwrinkled
your skin hooked tight over bone   i lay full
looselimbed   puppet on your string
eyes stretched on some inner play   you
were marble   an effigy before your own tomb
i gave up   i gave in

Now in the mango wind drifting
from island backyards   in the purpling of lilacs
on Memorial   at bridge hands in country lamplight
i remember you   your earlier times

young and laughing   i remember how silence
rewarded you   my father storming around
your stillness   then giving in

EPILOGUE

Rushing home from Calgary   my mother
dying   the forest roads lined with lilies
I see them mad   fluent   orange
and stop to capture this for her   later
in a mud green hospital room   though
gathered in huge bunches   dumped raw
in great stone jars   in the awesome
victorious silence   suddenly wildly
obscene   and stricken like this verse
extinguishing what is left of her
that is wild   and full of grace